This edition published by Barnes & Noble Inc.,
by arrangement with Carlton Books Ltd.

1999 Barnes & Noble Books

Text and puzzle copyright © 1997 British Mensa Limited
Design copyright © 1997 Carlton Books Limited

ISBN 0-7607-1664-1

10 9 8 7 6 5 4 3 2

Printed in Italy

MENSA MIND GAMES for KIDS

Nearly 200 mindbusting puzzles to fry your brain cells!

Carolyn Skitt

BARNES & NOBLE BOOKS
NEW YORK

CONTENTS

American Mensa Ltd is an organization for individuals who have one common trait: an IQ in the top 2% of the nation. Over 50,000 current members have found out how smart they are. This leaves room for an additional 4.5 million members in America alone. You may be one of them.

Looking for intellectual stimulation?

If you enjoy mental exercise, you'll find lots of good "workout programs" in the *Mensa Bulletin,* our national magazine. Voice your opinion in one of the newsletters published by each of our 150 local chapters. Learn from the many books and publications that are available to you as a member.

Looking for social interaction?

Are you a "people person," or would you like to meet other people with whom you feel comfortable? Then come to our local meetings, parties, and get-togethers. Participate in our lectures and debates. Attend our regional events and national gatherings. There's something happening on the Mensa calendar almost daily. So, you have lots of opportunities to meet people, exchange ideas, and make interesting new friends.

Looking for others who share your special interest?

Whether yours is as common as crossword puzzles or as esoteric as Egyptology, there's a Mensa Special Interest Group (SIG) for it.

Take the challenge. Find out how smart you really are. Contact American Mensa Ltd today and ask for a free brochure. We enjoy adding new members and ideas to our high-IQ organization.

American Mensa Ltd
1229 Corporate Drive West
Arlington
TX 76006-6103

Or, if you don't live in the USA and you'd like more details, you can contact: Mensa International, 15 The Ivories, 628 Northampton Street, London N1 2NY, England who will be happy to put you in touch with your own national Mensa.

AMERICAN MENSA LTD

I hope that you enjoy working through these puzzles as much as we have enjoyed compiling them. I would like to thank Bobby Raikhy and the staff at Mensa headquarters for their support and Carlton Books, who have made this publication possible.

You will find that some of the puzzles are particularly devious so here are a few clues which you may find useful:

1. Where words are converted to numbers look for Roman numeral values (I = 1, V = 5, X = 10, L = 50, C = 100, D = 500 and M = 1000). Also look for consonants and vowels having a value or alpha-numeric values, i.e., A = 1, B = 2 etc.

2. Average speeds can be calculated by dividing the total distance by the total time. If no time is given assume that the outward journey is completed in one hour and calculate the return time.

3. Intermeshing gears: calculate the number of teeth movements of the largest wheel. The others will then divide into this to give the number of revolutions of each of the wheels. The largest wheel moves clockwise, therefore the second largest will move anti-clockwise (or counterclockwise), the third will move clockwise and the fourth anti-clockwise (or counterclockwise).

4. In the cog questions look for the lowest common denominator.

5. With any of the recycling questions remember to keep dividing and using up all of the new remainders each time.

6. Where two or three words are merged together do not assume that all the words follow the same direction.

I hope these notes are helpful to you and GOOD LUCK!

PUZZLE 1

Some letters have been omitted from this alphabet.
Use the missing letters to form
the name of a planet.

ABCDFGHKLMNOQSVWXYZ

SEE ANSWER 60

PUZZLE 2

Which diagram should come next, A, B, C or D?

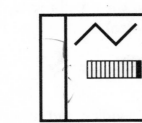 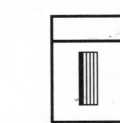 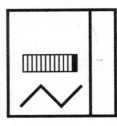

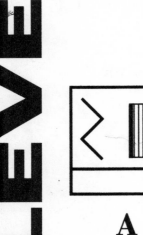  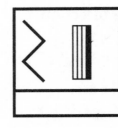 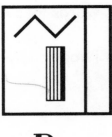

A   **B**   **C**   **D**

SEE ANSWER 7

PUZZLE 3

Move from square to touching square, including diagonally, to discover the name of a famous heavyweight boxer. There may be some letters left over. Who is it?

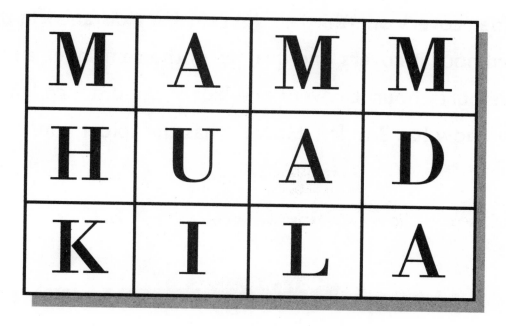

M	A	M	M
H	U	A	D
K	I	L	A

SEE ANSWER 52

PUZZLE 4

Each symbol in the diagram has a value. What number should replace the question mark?

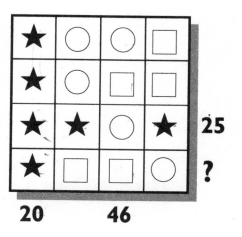

25

?

20   46

SEE ANSWER 15

PUZZLE 5

A spider is returning to its web to see if a tasty morsel is caught in it. In the first hour it covers one-quarter of the total distance to the web. In the second hour the spider covers one-third of the remaining distance. In the third hour it covers one-quarter of the remainder and in the fourth hour it covers one-half of the distance left. It now has 3 m left. How far has the spider run?

SEE ANSWER 44

PUZZLE 6

How many ways are there to score 25 on this dartboard using three darts only? Each dart lands in a segment and more than one dart can land in a segment, but no dart falls to the floor.

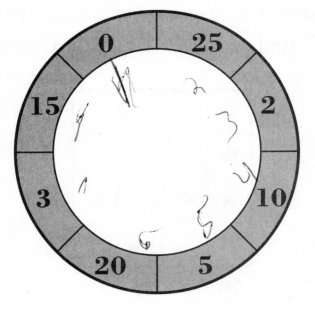

SEE ANSWER 23

A different letter is missing from each of the following words. When you have collected them, they will spell another word. What are all the words?

A?ULT   C?ACH   HEL?O   EM?TY

EIG?T   BAS?C   PIA?O

SEE ANSWER 36

PUZZLE 8

Which two boxes in the diagram contain the same symbols?

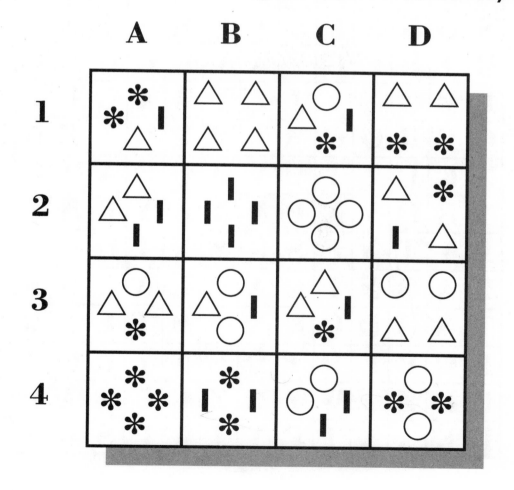

SEE ANSWER 31

LEVEL • EASY

11

The names of 10 film stars can be found in this grid on vertical, horizontal and diagonal lines.
Can you find them?

LEVEL • EASY

Robert De Niro	**Al Pacino**
James Dean	**Burt Reynolds**
Harrison Ford	**Julia Roberts**
Marilyn Monroe	**Meg Ryan**
Demi Moore	**Orson Welles**

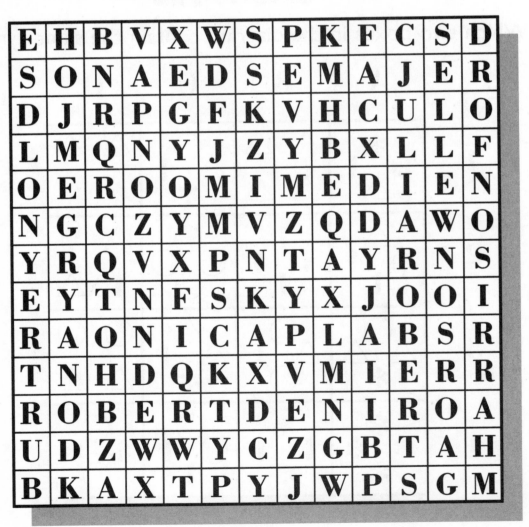

E	H	B	V	X	W	S	P	K	F	C	S	D
S	O	N	A	E	D	S	E	M	A	J	E	R
D	J	R	P	G	F	K	V	H	C	U	L	O
L	M	Q	N	Y	J	Z	Y	B	X	L	L	F
O	E	R	O	O	M	I	M	E	D	I	E	N
N	G	C	Z	Y	M	V	Z	Q	D	A	W	O
Y	R	Q	V	X	P	N	T	A	Y	R	N	S
E	Y	T	N	F	S	K	Y	X	J	O	O	I
R	A	O	N	I	C	A	P	L	A	B	S	R
T	N	H	D	Q	K	X	V	M	I	E	R	R
R	O	B	E	R	T	D	E	N	I	R	O	A
U	D	Z	W	W	Y	C	Z	G	B	T	A	H
B	K	A	X	T	P	Y	J	W	P	S	G	M

SEE ANSWER 28

12

PUZZLE 10

In a mass pie-eating contest, Adam ate 8 more pies than Belinda, and Belinda ate 7 less than Chris. Eddie ate 2 more pies than Dawn, and Chris ate 1 more than Eddie. Belinda and Eddie ate 14 pies between them. How many pies were eaten in total?

SEE ANSWER 39

PUZZLE 11

By taking a segment and finding its pair in the diagram, the names of four American states can be found. Which states are they?

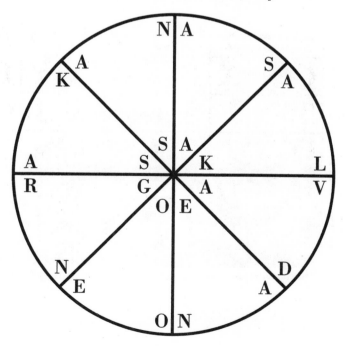

SEE ANSWER 20

LEVEL • EASY

PUZZLE 12

Robert from Rouen has FF2.64 in his piggy bank. It is made up of an equal number of four coins of different denominations from 1 centime, 5 centimes, 10 centimes, 20 centimes, 50 centimes and 1 franc. Any four of the above coins may be in the piggy bank. How many of each coin does Robert have and what are their respective values?

SEE ANSWER 47

PUZZLE 13

There is a logic in the distances to the cities shown on this sign. How far should it be to Melbourne?

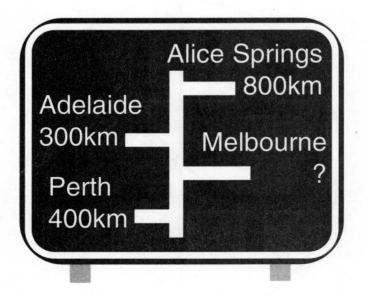

SEE ANSWER 12

If a slice is taken from the following object as indicated what view would you see from above?

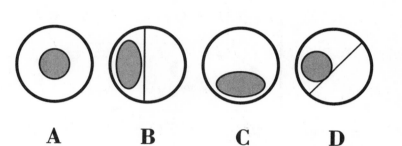

Sphere **A** **B** **C** **D**

SEE ANSWER 55

PUZZLE 15

Rearrange each of the following groups to find four associated words. What are they?

SNUVE

STUNAR

SRAM

TOLUP

SEE ANSWER 4

LEVEL · EASY

15

PUZZLE 16

What number should replace the question mark?

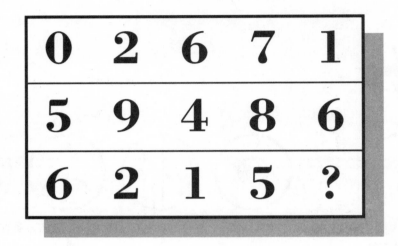

0	2	6	7	1
5	9	4	8	6
6	2	1	5	?

SEE ANSWER 8

PUZZLE 17

The names of three British classic car manufacturers have been merged together here. Who are they?

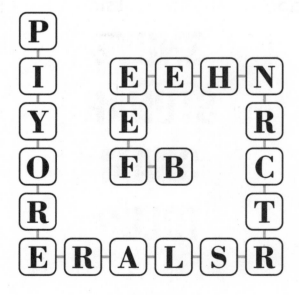

SEE ANSWER 59

PUZZLE 18

Clock A was correct at midnight but began to lose 4 minutes per hour from that moment. It stopped an hour ago showing the time on clock B. The clock runs for less than 24 hours. What is the correct time now?

A
00.00

B
03.44

SEE ANSWER 16

PUZZLE 19

Start at the top left corner and move down the first column, up the second, down the third column and so on. In which direction should the missing arrow point?

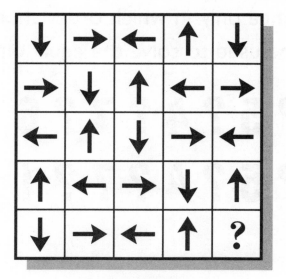

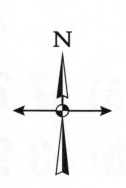

N

SEE ANSWER 51

PUZZLE 20

How many squares can you see in the shape below?

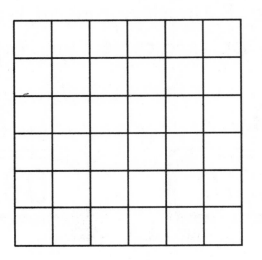

SEE ANSWER 24

PUZZLE 21

Assume you are using a basic calculator and press the numbers in order replacing each question mark with a mathematical sign. Plus, minus, multiply and divide can be used once only. In which order should they be used to solve the equations?

a) **7 ? 5 ? 4 ? 7 ? 6 = 15**

b) **3 ? 5 ? 4 ? 7 ? 1 = 25**

SEE ANSWER 43

When a bar of soap has been used a small piece remains. An old miser knows that from 6 slivers of soap he can make another bar. If he has 176 small pieces of soap how many full bars can he possibly make? Remember that a new piece of soap can be reused when it becomes small.

SEE ANSWER 32

2E	2B	4A	1C	5E		2D	3C	5D	1E
					■				
5A	3C	1D	5C	1B		5B	4E	2B	3D

The wordframe above, when filled with the correct letters, will give the name of a singer. The letters are arranged in the grid below. There are two possible letters to fill each square of the wordframe, one correct, the other incorrect.

Who is the singer?

	A	B	C	D	E
1	F	T	N	G	S
2	K	S	L	B	D
3	C	Q	I	P	J
4	A	U	W	E	O
5	M	R	H	V	A

SEE ANSWER 35

LEVEL • EASY

19

What number is missing from this series?

1, 5, ?, 50, 100, 500

SEE ANSWER 40

SEE ANSWER 40

PUZZLE 25

How many triangles can you see in the shape below?

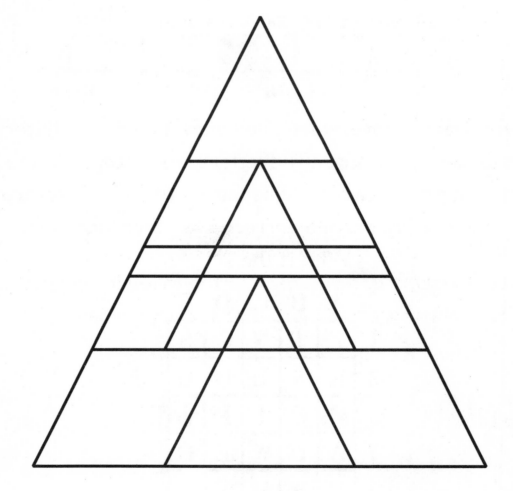

SEE ANSWER 27

PUZZLE 26

Move from square to touching square, including diagonals, to
discover the name of a famous glamorous actress from the past.
There may be some letters left over. Who is it?

O	M	N	Y	J
R	N	L	R	M
T	O	E	I	A

SEE ANSWER 48

PUZZLE 27

Place the same letter in each of the following groups and
rearrange each group to form a currency.
What are the four currencies?

CNFR   ROLLD   DRN   STEEP

SEE ANSWER 19

LEVEL • EASY

21

Which of these is not a view of the same box?

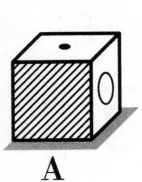

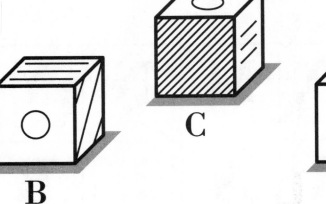

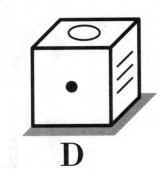

A

B

C

D

SEE ANSWER 56

PUZZLE 29

Scales 1 and 2 are in perfect balance. How many As are required to balance Scale 3?

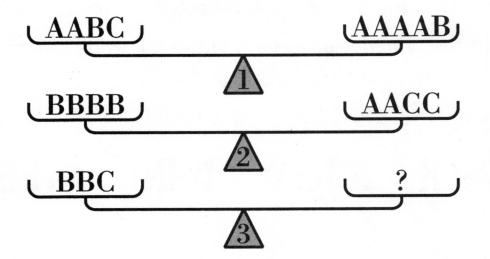

AABC · AAAAB

1

BBBB · AACC

2

BBC · ?

3

SEE ANSWER 11

22

PUZZLE 30

Move from square to touching square, including diagonals, in this grid to find the longest possible word. There may be some letters left over. What is the word?

V	T	I	I	T
K	N	E	O	A
L	A	N	R	N

SEE ANSWER I

PUZZLE 31

Moving from the left-hand hexagon progress from left to right, not up or down. What are the maximum and minimum scores possible, and how many ways are there to score 40?

SEE ANSWER 3

LEVEL · EASY

PUZZLE 32

Rearrange these number tiles, in a 3 x 3 grid as shown,
so that each pair of adjacent numbers add up to 10.
The central square does not change position.

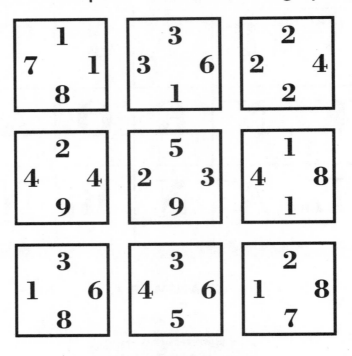

SEE ANSWER 9

PUZZLE 33

If a slice is taken from the following object as indicated
what view would you see from above?

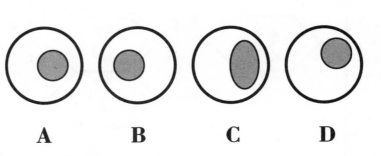

cone   A   B   C   D

SEE ANSWER 62

What are the missing numbers ?

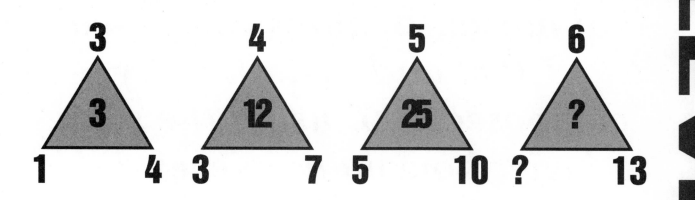

SEE ANSWER 17

PUZZLE 35

An array of 64 lights change at different rates. Red lights turn green after 5 seconds. Green lights turn blue after 10 seconds and blue lights turn red after 20 seconds. When the lights are switched on 32 are red, 20 are green and 12 are blue. After 30 seconds how many each of red, green and blue will be displayed?

SEE ANSWER 54

LEVEL • EASY

If Chopin composed 101 pieces of music, Brahms composed 1,000 and Tchaikovsky composed 106, using the same logic, how many pieces did Liszt compose?

SEE ANSWER 25

PUZZLE 37

Some letters have been omitted from this alphabet. Use the missing letters to form the name of a car manufacturer.

BCDFHIJMPQRTUXYZ

LEVEL • EASY

SEE ANSWER 46

Two words have been omitted from this sentence. They are anagrams of each other. What are the two words?

If my ---- of soup is too hot,
I will ---- on it to cool it down.

SEE ANSWER 33

PUZZLE 39

A five-letter word can be added to the end of the four words on the left to create a new word in each case. The same five-letter word can also be added to the front of the four words to the right and this will also make four new words. What is this five-letter word?

Fly   **Back**

Wall   **?**   **Chase**

News   **Mate**

Waste   **Work**

SEE ANSWER 38

PUZZLE 40

How many triangles can you see in the shape below?

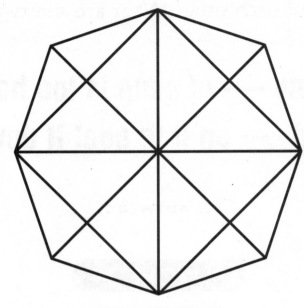

SEE ANSWER 41

PUZZLE 41

Which two boxes in the diagram contain the same symbols?

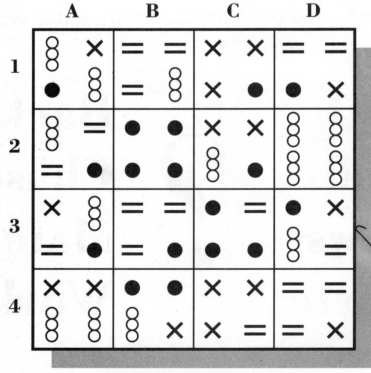

SEE ANSWER 30

How many ways are there to score 60 on this dartboard using three darts only? Each dart lands in a segment and more than one may land in the same segment, but no dart falls to the floor.

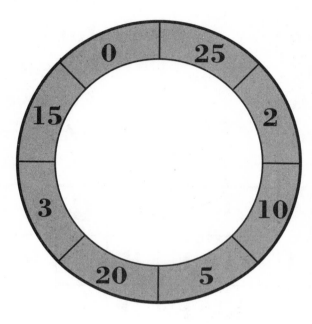

SEE ANSWER 49

The following four words have their letters mixed up. Three of them have something in common and other is related but definitely different. What are the words and which is the odd one out?

FECEFO   ATE   RAGSU   LKMI

SEE ANSWER 22

LEVEL • EASY

The names of ten American presidents can be found in this grid on vertical, horizontal and diagonal lines. Can you find them?

LEVEL • EASY

Carter	**Lincoln**
Clinton	**Nixon**
Ford	**Reagan**
Johnson	**Roosevelt**
Kennedy	**Washington**

W	Y	V	D	B	K	G	D	J	R
N	A	G	A	E	R	Y	R	O	E
B	Z	S	K	F	D	C	O	H	T
J	D	H	H	E	L	S	F	N	R
C	H	F	N	I	E	H	B	S	A
K	V	N	N	V	N	F	C	O	C
B	E	T	E	J	I	G	T	N	G
K	O	L	V	F	X	Z	T	W	J
N	T	G	C	J	O	V	G	O	C
W	N	L	O	C	N	I	L	Z	N

SEE ANSWER 57

Here is a simple word square. The words read the same across and down. The first word has been given to you and the letters for the other two are below. How should the completed box look?

E E R Y

SEE ANSWER 14

You are visiting America and in your pocket you have $6.02. It is made up of an equal number of four coins of different denominations: $1, 50c, 25c, 10c, 5c and 1c. How many of each of the four coins do you have and what are their respective values?

SEE ANSWER 5

LEVEL · EASY

How far it is to Jellystone on this unusual signpost?

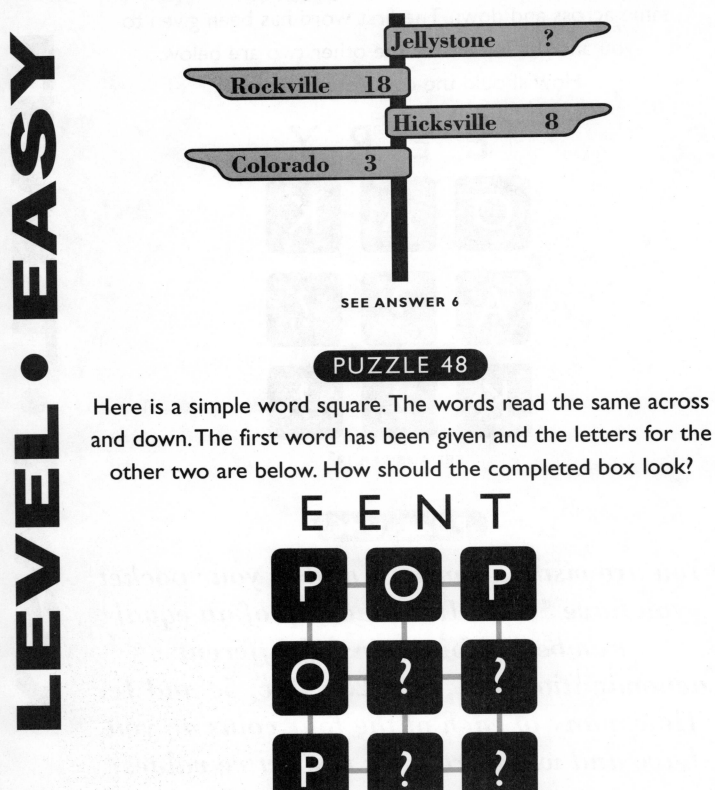

Jellystone ?

Rockville 18

Hicksville 8

Colorado 3

SEE ANSWER 6

PUZZLE 48

Here is a simple word square. The words read the same across and down. The first word has been given and the letters for the other two are below. How should the completed box look?

E E N T

P O P

O ? ?

P ? ?

SEE ANSWER 13

LEVEL • EASY

PUZZLE 49

The names of two rock bands are merged together here.
Who are they?

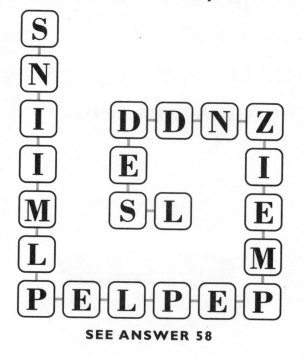

SEE ANSWER 58

PUZZLE 50

Clock A was correct at midnight but began to lose 2 minutes
per hour from that moment. It stopped 2 hours ago, showing
the time on clock B. The clock runs for less than 24 hours.
What is the correct time now?

SEE ANSWER 21

LEVEL • EASY

33

PUZZLE 51

In a book about scientists Isaac Newton is featured on page 101, Charles Darwin is on page 651 and Albert Einstein is on page 52. On which page is Georg Simon Ohm featured?

SEE ANSWER 50

PUZZLE 52

If a slice is taken from the pyramid below as indicated what view would you see from above?

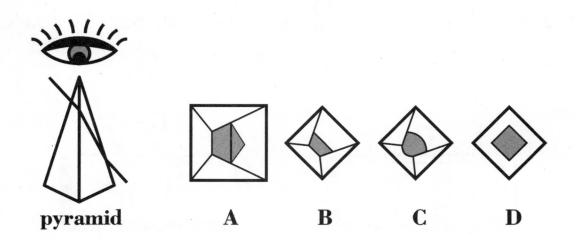

pyramid   A   B   C   D

SEE ANSWER 29

PUZZLE 53

2A 1C 3A 4E 4D 3C 4B 1A 3B 5A 3E

☐ ☐ ☐ ☐ ☐ ☐ ☐ ☐ ☐ ☐ ☐

2E 2B 5B 3D 4A 1E 5C 2E 1D 4D 5D

The wordframe above, when filled with the correct letters, will give the name of a river. The letters are arranged in the grid below. There are two possible letters to fill each square of the wordframe, one correct, the other incorrect. What is the river?

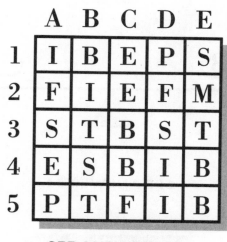

	A	B	C	D	E
1	I	B	E	P	S
2	F	I	E	F	M
3	S	T	B	S	T
4	E	S	B	I	B
5	P	T	F	I	B

SEE ANSWER 42

PUZZLE 54

Place the same letter in each of the following groups and rearrange each group to form the name of an artist.
Who are the three artists?

STANBLEC   SCASPI   MENT

SEE ANSWER 37

LEVEL • EASY

PUZZLE 55

Scales 1 and 2 are in perfect balance. How many C's are required balance Scale 3?

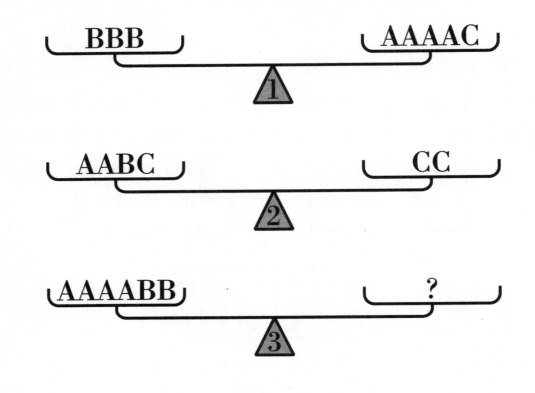

SEE ANSWER 34

PUZZLE 56

Some letters have been omitted from this alphabet. Use the missing letters to form the name of a state in America.

ABCDFGHIJLMPQSTUVXZ

SEE ANSWER 45

Move from square to touching square, including diagonals, to discover the name of a pop star. Who is it?

SEE ANSWER 26

Which two boxes in the diagram contain the same symbols?

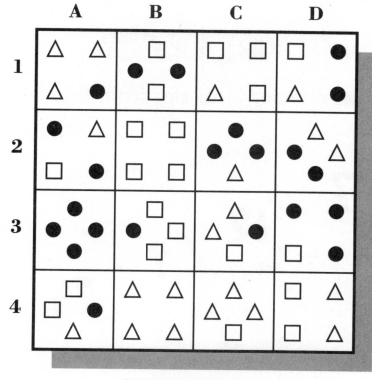

SEE ANSWER 53

Each like symbol in the diagram has the same value.
What number should replace the question mark?

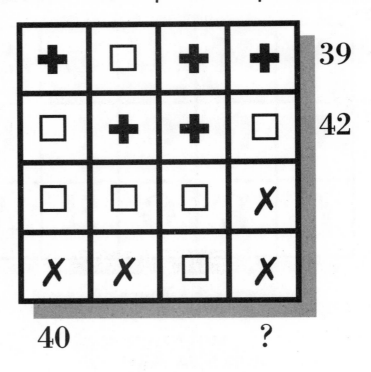

39

42

40   ?

SEE ANSWER 18

PUZZLE 60

What number is missing from this series?

5

7

12

?

31

50

SEE ANSWER 61

38

What time should be shown on the fourth clock?

SEE ANSWER 10

PUZZLE 62

Can you calculate the values of the question marks in the diagram below?

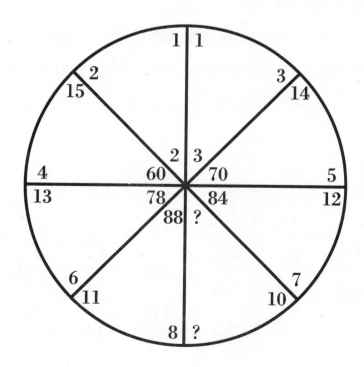

SEE ANSWER 2

LEVEL • EASY

PUZZLE 1

Some letters have been omitted from this alphabet.
Use the missing letters to form the name of a city in the United
States of America.

B C E F G H I J K M
Q S U V W X Y Z

SEE ANSWER 32

PUZZLE 2

Moving from the left-hand hexagon progress from left to right,
but not up or down, to an adjacent hexagon. What are the
maximum and minimum scores possible, and how many ways
are there to score 171?

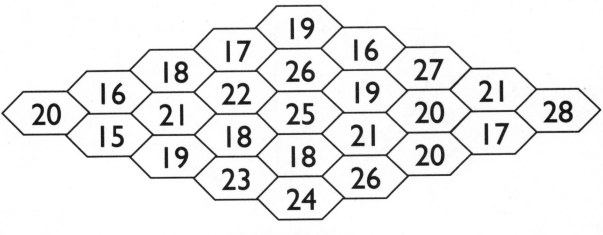

SEE ANSWER 25

PUZZLE 3

Move from square to touching square, including diagonals, to discover the name of a film star. Not every letter may be used. Who is it?

O R	T	R
I	D E	O
N	E B	R

SEE ANSWER 48

PUZZLE 4

Work out how much time has elapsed between each clock shown. What time should the fifth clock show?

1   2   3   4   5

LEVEL • MEDIUM

PUZZLE 5

A swimmer sets herself a task of swimming a certain number of lengths of the pool in five days. On the first day she covers one fifth of the total. The next day she swims one third of the remaining lengths. On the third day she covers half of the remaining lengths and on the fourth day she swims one quarter of the remainder. She still has 24 lengths left.

How many lengths has she swum?

SEE ANSWER 64

PUZZLE 6

How many ways are there to score 18 on this dartboard using three darts only? Each dart lands in a segment, and more than one can land in the same segment, but no dart falls to the floor.

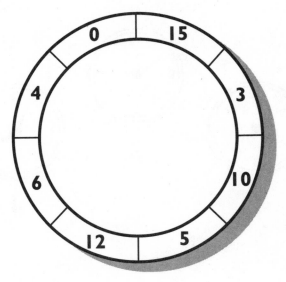

SEE ANSWER 41

PUZZLE 7

Which number is the odd one out in this series?

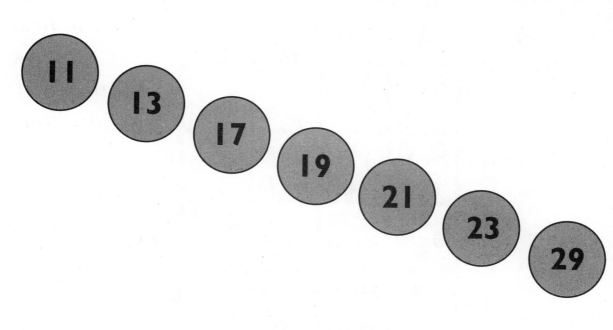

SEE ANSWER 16

PUZZLE 8

Andy is 7 years older than Beattie
and Beattie is 5 years younger than Carrie.
Elsie is 2 years older than Danni
and Carrie is a year older than Elsie.
Beattie's and Elsie's ages added together are 20.

How old is each person?

SEE ANSWER 57

Which two boxes in the diagram contain the same symbols?

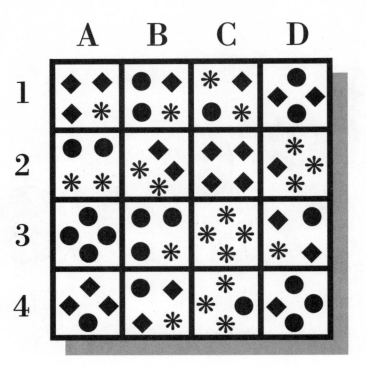

A   B   C   D

1   2   3   4

SEE ANSWER 40

PUZZLE 10

At an airport 8 people are waiting for a flight to Virginia, 103 are going to Illinois and 152 are waiting to fly to California.

How many people are waiting for a flight to Texas?

SEE ANSWER 33

LEVEL · MEDIUM

The names of 10 singers can be found in this grid on vertical, horizontal and diagonal lines. Can you find them?

Nat King Cole   **Tom Jones**
Phil Collins   **John Lennon**
Neil Diamond   **Paul McCartney**
Janet Jackson   **George Michael**
Elton John   **Frank Sinatra**

A	R	T	A	N	I	S	K	N	A	R	F	P
N	E	I	L	D	I	A	M	O	N	D	A	H
N	O	N	N	E	L	N	H	O	J	U	B	I
B	C	N	H	O	J	N	O	T	L	E	T	L
K	H	V	X	F	P	Y	B	M	J	A	O	C
H	A	Y	H	B	K	Z	C	V	Q	F	M	O
C	W	P	Z	D	Z	C	X	G	W	D	J	L
X	Q	F	X	K	A	J	Z	K	Y	K	O	L
G	K	W	R	R	V	Q	X	P	Q	S	N	I
D	N	A	T	K	I	N	G	C	O	L	E	N
J	V	N	J	Q	W	Y	A	Z	J	G	S	S
L	E	A	H	C	I	M	E	G	R	O	E	G
Y	J	A	N	E	T	J	A	C	K	S	O	N

SEE ANSWER 1

PUZZLE 12

Way back in the mists of time, when your parents hadn't even been born, the Rolling Stones had 42 hit records, the Beatles had 28 and Elvis Presley had 32.
How many hit records did Buddy Holly have?

SEE ANSWER 8

After a shopping trip to London, you have a selection of the
following coins in your pocket:
1p, 5p, 10p, 20p, 50p and £1.
The coins total £10.26 and this total is made up of an equal
number of four coins of different denominations.

How many of each coin are there
and what are their respective values?

SEE ANSWER 56

By taking a segment and finding its pair in the diagram the name
of a car manufacturer can be found.
Which four Oriental car manufacturers are concealed here?

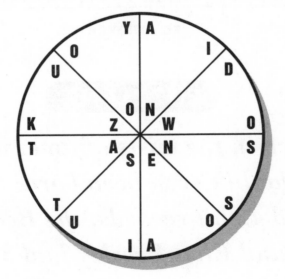

SEE ANSWER 49

The names of three scientists are written here, unfortunately the vowels have been missed out. Replace the vowels to discover the three names. Who are they?

SCNWTN   LBRTNSTN

LSPSTR

SEE ANSWER 36

PUZZLE 16

What number should replace the question mark?

2	1	0	2
1	6	3	0
5	2	4	4
3	8	6	?

SEE ANSWER 24

LEVEL • MEDIUM

47

PUZZLE 17

Three cities in Australia and New Zealand are merged together here. Which are they?

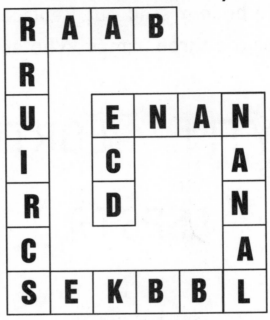

SEE ANSWER 47

PUZZLE 18

Each like letter in the diagram has the same value. What number should replace the question mark?

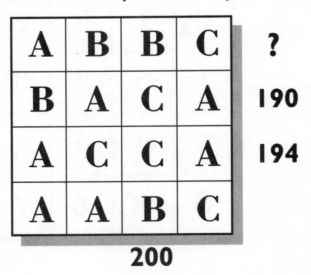

A	B	B	C	?
B	A	C	A	190
A	C	C	A	194
A	A	B	C	

200

SEE ANSWER 28

Clock A was correct at midnight but began to lose 2½ minutes per hour from that moment. It stopped 2 hours ago showing the time on clock B. The clock runs for less than 24 hours. What is the correct time now?

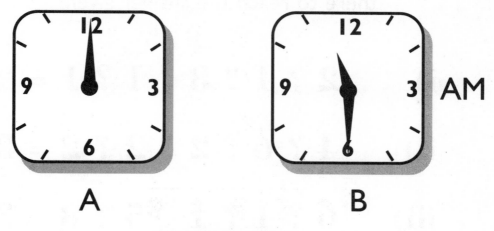

A   B

SEE ANSWER 55

PUZZLE 20

The arrows spiral clockwise from the top left corner. In which direction should the missing arrow point?

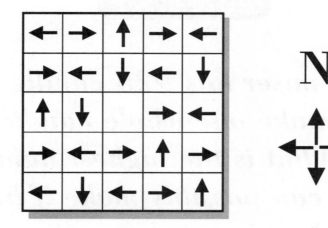

SEE ANSWER 12

Assume you are using a basic calculator and you press the numbers in order, replacing each question mark with a mathematical sign. Plus, minus, multiply and divide can each be used once only. How many different ways are there to reach the answer given?

i) $\quad 2 ? 1 ? 8 ? 1 ? 1 = 9$

ii) $\quad 4 ? 6 ? 2 ? 2 ? 2 = 8$

iii) $\quad 6 ? 1 ? 1 ? 5 ? 8 = 33$

iv) $\quad 7 ? 6 ? 9 ? 5 ? 5 = 10.5$

SEE ANSWER 63

That old miser has 925 candle stubs. He can make one whole candle from 7 ends. What is the highest number of candles he can possibly make if he carries on burning and recycling?

SEE ANSWER 52

PUZZLE 23

Four interlinked gear wheels with arrows on them start in the position shown below. If the largest wheel is rotated clockwise for 6 rotations, what directions will the arrows point on the 3 smaller wheels. The number of teeth on each wheel is given on the diagram.

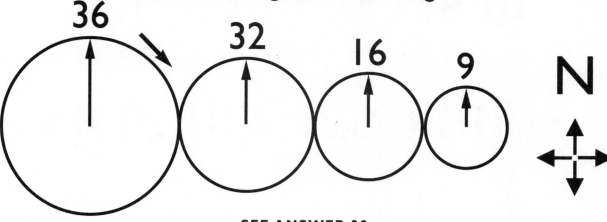

SEE ANSWER 39

PUZZLE 24

By taking a segment and finding its pair in the diagram the name of an American city can be found. Which four American cities are concealed here?

SEE ANSWER 15

PUZZLE 25

Place the same two letters in each of the following groups and rearrange each group to give a European city.
What are the four cities?

BESPUD KRUFFRN

SCHERMEN CHUBERS

SEE ANSWER 31

PUZZLE 26

Which of these is not a view of the same box?

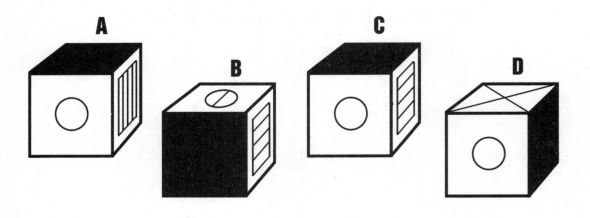

SEE ANSWER 20

Can you calculate the values of A and B in the segments?

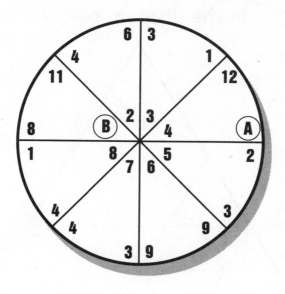

SEE ANSWER 4

PUZZLE 28

Rearrange these number tiles, in a 3 x 3 grid as shown, so that each pair of adjacent numbers adds up to 10.

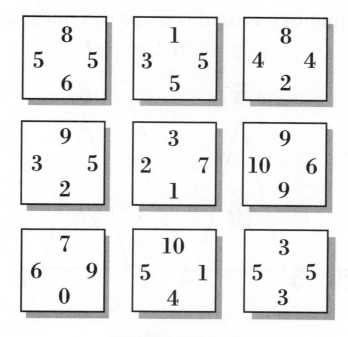

SEE ANSWER 44

LEVEL • MEDIUM

PUZZLE 29

Can you see how many triangles can be found
in the diagram below?

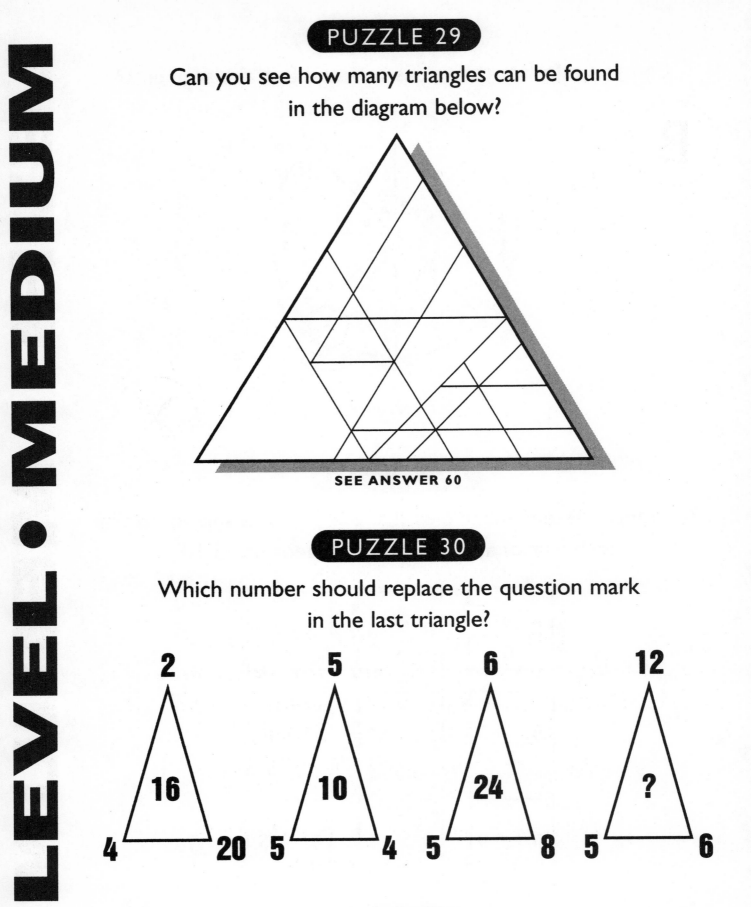

SEE ANSWER 60

PUZZLE 30

Which number should replace the question mark
in the last triangle?

2
16
4   20

5
10
5   4

6
24
5   8

12
?
5   6

SEE ANSWER 17

Which letter is missing in this sequence?

B F J M Q ? X

SEE ANSWER 7

PUZZLE 32

*A car travels at 100 km/h for
1 minute and then 75 km/h for 40 seconds.
It then travels for 5 more minutes and
the average overall speed
for the total journey is 60 km/h.*

*What speed was the car doing
in the last 5 minutes?*

SEE ANSWER 23

LEVEL • MEDIUM

LEVEL • MEDIUM

PUZZLE 33

Some letters have been missed out of this alphabet. Use the missing letters to form the name of a famous professional golfer.

BEGHJMPQRSTUVWXYZ

SEE ANSWER 42

PUZZLE 34

Move from square to touching square to discover the name of an English poet. Not every letter may have been used. Who is it?

W	L	M	A	O
L	I	I	W	R
R	W	S	D	K
O	T	H	Z	B

SEE ANSWER 61

PUZZLE 35

Work out how much time has elapsed between each clock shown. What time should the fifth clock show?

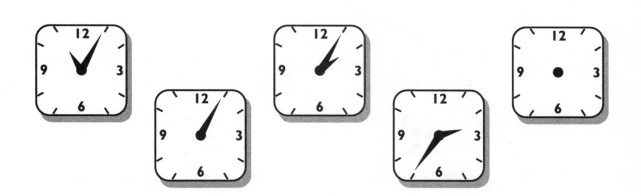

SEE ANSWER 10

PUZZLE 36

On the first day of a sightseeing tour one-seventh of the total journey is completed. On the second day the bus travels one-third of the remaining distance. The following day one-quarter of the remaining distance is covered and on the fourth day the bus travels half of the distance left. There are still 75 miles of the journey left.

How far has the bus gone?

SEE ANSWER 53

LEVEL • MEDIUM

How many ways are there to score 55 on this dartboard using three darts only? Each dart lands in a segment and more than one may land in a segment, but no dart falls to the floor.

SEE ANSWER 18

PUZZLE 38

A girl goes walking on a hill. On the way up the hill she averages 2 km per hour, but on the way back down she averages 8 km per hour. What was her overall speed?

SEE ANSWER 45

PUZZLE 39

Over a soccer season Angela scores 23 more goals than Betty and Betty scores 16 less than Christy. Eva scores 6 goals more than Daisy and Christy scores 5 more than Eva. Betty and Eva score 17 goals between them.

Who scores what and how many goals are scored in total?

SEE ANSWER 26

PUZZLE 40

Which two boxes in the diagram contain the same symbols?

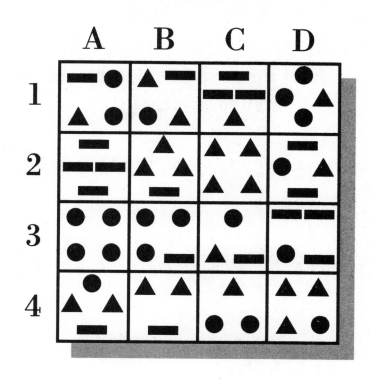

SEE ANSWER 5

PUZZLE 41

The names of 10 cities in the USA can be found in this grid on vertical, horizontal and diagonal lines.
Can you find them?

Austin
Detroit
Boston
Miami
Chicago
Milwaukee
Cincinnati
Phoenix
Dallas
Savannah

M	I	L	W	A	U	K	E	E	I
A	B	C	J	X	K	X	H	T	P
T	U	Q	S	A	L	L	A	D	H
I	Q	S	Z	H	M	N	N	C	O
O	X	F	T	I	N	Z	N	G	E
R	H	B	A	I	V	B	A	H	N
T	P	M	C	W	N	Q	V	C	I
E	I	N	Q	C	J	K	A	J	X
D	I	B	X	N	O	T	S	O	B
C	H	I	C	A	G	O	Z	W	G

SEE ANSWER 50

PUZZLE 42

By taking a sector and finding its pair in the diagram the names of three sportsmen can be found.
Who are they?

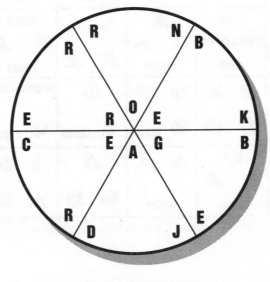

SEE ANSWER 29

PUZZLE 43

Helga from Berlin has DM10.44 in her piggy bank. It is made up of an equal number of four coins of different denominations: 1 Deutschmark, 50 pfennig, 20 pfennig, 10 pfennig, 5 pfennig and 1 pfennig. How many of each of the four coins are there and what are their respective values?

SEE ANSWER 2

PUZZLE 44

What number should replace the question mark?

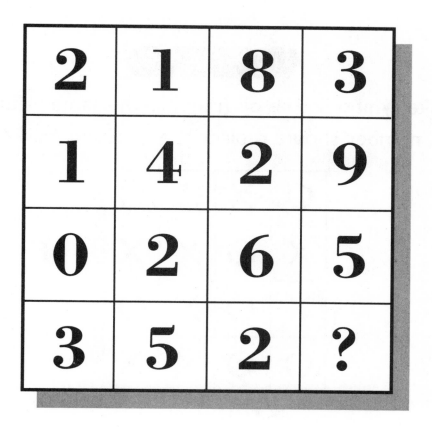

2	1	8	3
1	4	2	9
0	2	6	5
3	5	2	?

SEE ANSWER 21

PUZZLE 45

Rearrange these number tiles in a 3 x 3 grid so that each pair of adjacent numbers add up to 11.

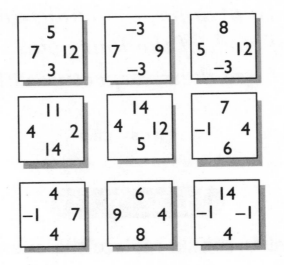

SEE ANSWER 34

PUZZLE 46

Each like symbol in the diagram has the same value. What number should replace the question mark?

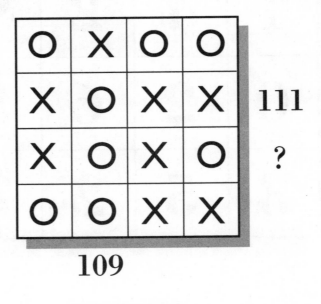

SEE ANSWER 13

Clock A was correct at midnight but began to lose 3 minutes each hour from that moment. It stopped 1½ hours ago showing the time on clock B. The clock runs for less than 24 hours. What is the correct time now?

A

PM

B

SEE ANSWER 58

Aileen has $23 more than Bruce and Bruce has $18 less than Charlotte. Emily has $12 more than Denis and Charlotte has $2 more than Emily. Bruce and Emily have $40 between them. How much money do they have in total?

SEE ANSWER 37

LEVEL • MEDIUM

PUZZLE 49

Four interlinked gear wheels with arrows on them start in the position shown below. If the largest wheel is rotated clockwise for 5 rotations, in what direction will the arrow point on the smallest wheel? The number of teeth on each wheel is given on the diagram.

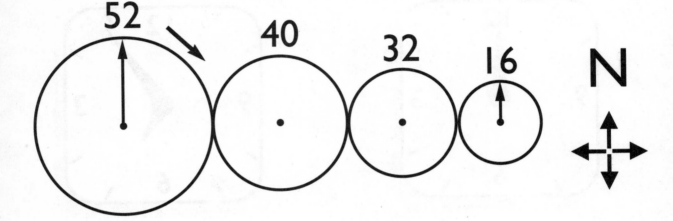

SEE ANSWER 62

PUZZLE 50

Which numbers should replace the question marks in these triangles?

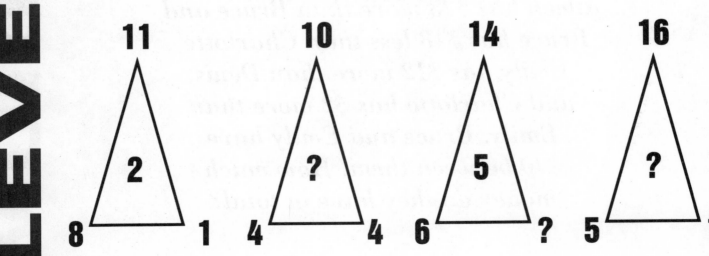

SEE ANSWER 3

PUZZLE 51

2D	3D	4D	5C		5A	2B	5E	1A	2D	2B	2C
1E	1C	4A	4D		2E	4B	4B	5C	1C	1D	3C

The wordframe above, when filled with the correct letters, will give the name of a British actor. The letters are arranged in the grid below. There are two possible letters to fill each square of the wordframe, one correct, the other incorrect.
Who is the actor?

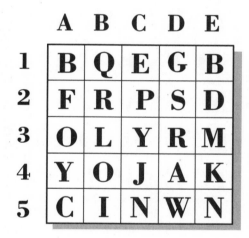

	A	B	C	D	E
1	B	Q	E	G	B
2	F	R	P	S	D
3	O	L	Y	R	M
4	Y	O	J	A	K
5	C	I	N	W	N

SEE ANSWER 59

PUZZLE 52

One letter is missing from each of the following groups. Replace the letter and rearrange each group to form the name of four sports stars. Who are they?

YZETKG AVANTALIVO STICHIE MAPASS

SEE ANSWER 11

2C	1D	4B	1E	1E		3D	2A	4C	5B	1A	5E	4D
2B	3E	4A	5D	2D		1B	5E	3A	2C	2D	4C	3B

The wordframe above, when filled with the correct letters, will give the name of an actress. The letters are arranged in the grid below. There are two possible letters to fill each square of the wordframe, one correct, the other incorrect.

Who is she?

	A	B	C	D	E
1	F	R	N	C	A
2	O	V	J	R	H
3	M	S	W	G	U
4	L	X	B	Q	K
5	D	E	P	I	T

SEE ANSWER 38

PUZZLE 54

In an electronic assembly containing 2,000 untested components, 20% of the components have a 0.5% defect rate, 40% have a 0.25% defect rate, 10% have a 1.0% defect rate and the balance have no defects. If all of the parts are used in production without being tested first, how many defects would there be in the assembled products?

SEE ANSWER 19

PUZZLE 55

Rearrange these number tiles, in a 3 x 3 grid as shown, so that each pair of adjacent numbers add up to 12.

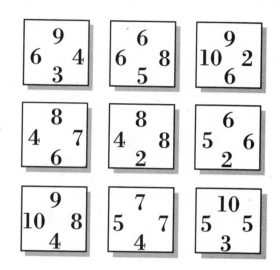

SEE ANSWER 46

PUZZLE 56

Three cities in the Orient are merged together here. Which are they?

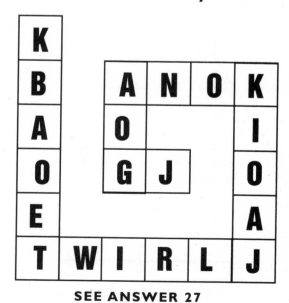

SEE ANSWER 27

67

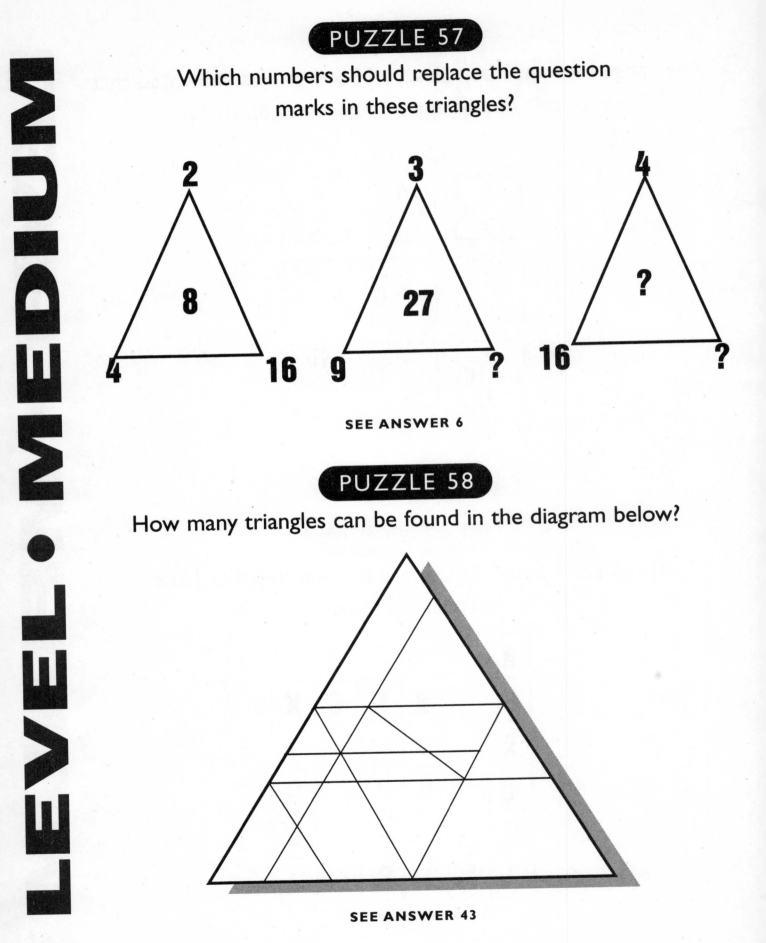

PUZZLE 57

Which numbers should replace the question marks in these triangles?

SEE ANSWER 6

PUZZLE 58

How many triangles can be found in the diagram below?

SEE ANSWER 43

In a school test Annie scored
75 more marks than Bertie and
Bertie attained 68 marks less than Charlie.
Ernie achieved 27 more than Donny and
Charlie scored 26 more than Ernie.
Bertie and Ernie achieved 82 marks between them.
How many marks did each child score?

SEE ANSWER 22

PUZZLE 60

By taking a sector and finding its pair in the diagram three
currencies can be found. What are they?

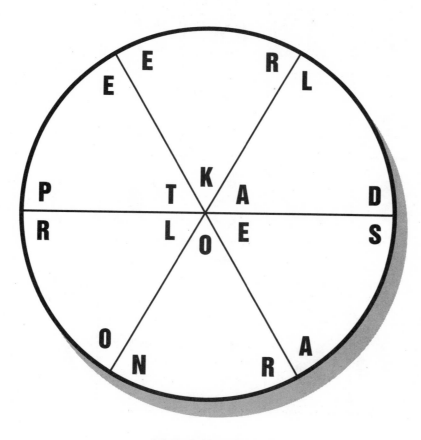

SEE ANSWER 35

The letters of four American states are written here but their order has been mixed up and one letter is missing from each. Rearrange the letters and replace the missing letters. The missing letters will give the name of a fifth state when placed together. What are the five states?

ZINARA   MOLAKOA   DIANNA   GROEN

SEE ANSWER 14

PUZZLE 62

What number should replace the question mark?

9	4	6	8	5
3	7	6	3	7
8	5	5	9	4
4	6	7	2	8
10	3	?	7	6

SEE ANSWER 51

LEVEL • MEDIUM

Our friend, the miser has 513 candle stubs. He
can make one new candle from 9 ends. What is
the highest number of whole candles he
can make if he continues to reuse the ends?

SEE ANSWER 30

PUZZLE 64

Two intermeshing gears are shown below. The large gear has
400 teeth and the smaller one has 384 teeth. How many
clockwise rotations will it take the large gear to make the
arrow on the smaller gear point directly East
when the large gear points North?

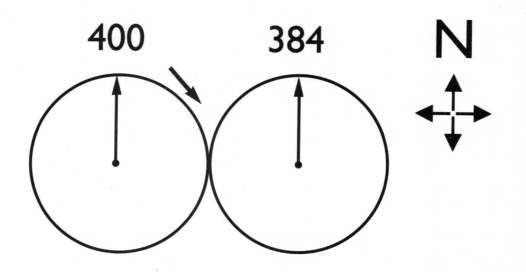

400   384   N

LEVEL • MEDIUM

PUZZLE 1

Some letters have been omitted from this alphabet.
Use the missing letters to form the name of
a British author.

BFGHJKMNPQTUVXYZ

SEE ANSWER 11

PUZZLE 2

Which diagram should come next?

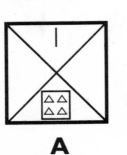 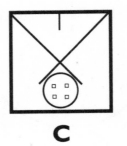 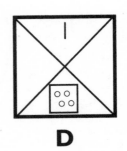

A   **B**   **C**   **D**

SEE ANSWER 43

PUZZLE 3

Move from square to touching square to discover the name of a former British Prime Minister. Who is it?

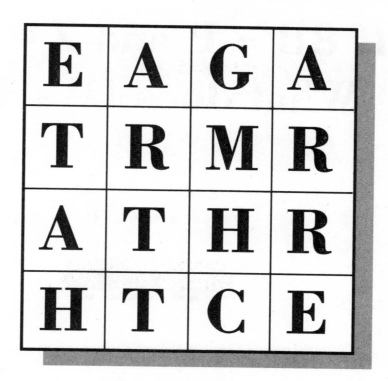

SEE ANSWER 50

PUZZLE 4

Work out how much time has elapsed between each clock shown. What time should the fifth clock show?

SEE ANSWER 27

LEVEL · TOUGH

73

If 8B = P and Z – J = P, What does $D^2 \div P = $?

SEE ANSWER 40

PUZZLE 6

How many squares and rectangles can you find in this puzzle?

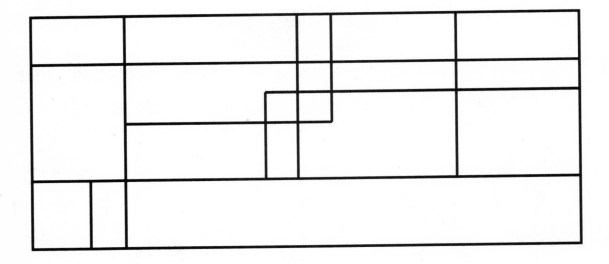

SEE ANSWER 57

LEVEL · TOUGH

PUZZLE 7

A supermarket delivery agent delivers baked beans to four stores and then returns to the warehouse. The driver delivers one-quarter of the load to the first store, then one-half of the remainder at the next store, then one-quarter of the remainder at the third store and one-third of what is left at the fourth store. The delivery agent has 480 cans of beans to go back to the warehouse. How many cans of beans did the driver start with and how many have been delivered?

SEE ANSWER 31

PUZZLE 8

Which two boxes in the diagram have the same symbols?

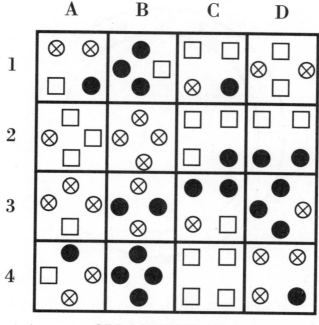

SEE ANSWER 12

PUZZLE 9

A number of companies in US cities took part in a fun day. In Las Vegas 45 companies took part, in Annapolis 49 took part and in Kansas City 99 companies took part. How many companies in Charleston took part?

SEE ANSWER 4

PUZZLE 10

How many ways are there to score 12 on this dartboard using three darts only? Each dart lands in a segment and more than one can land in the same segment, but no dart falls to the floor.

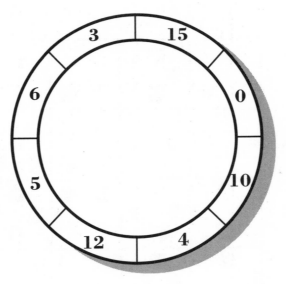

SEE ANSWER 35

PUZZLE 11

In a garden there are 6 more yellow rose bushes than orange ones and there are 4 less orange rose bushes than pink ones. There are 2 more red ones than white ones and 1 more pink rose bush than red. If the number of orange rose bushes is added to the number of red ones the total is 7. How many bushes are there in total?

SEE ANSWER 52

PUZZLE 12

The names of 10 composers can be found in this grid on vertical, horizontal and diagonal lines. Can you find them?

Bach
Beethoven
Borodin
Mendelssohn
Puccini
Rachmaninoff
Rossini
Schoenberg
Schubert
Strauss

A	J	L	B	S	O	P	H	F	N	K	F
H	N	F	C	S	S	X	Q	N	H	F	A
B	V	H	R	Y	M	U	E	C	O	V	S
N	C	W	O	D	K	V	A	N	H	C	C
I	F	V	G	S	O	B	I	R	H	B	H
D	R	Q	X	H	S	N	J	O	T	F	U
O	Z	O	T	Y	A	L	E	B	V	S	B
R	J	E	S	M	G	N	E	Z	D	G	E
O	E	W	H	S	B	Z	Z	D	Q	K	R
B	T	C	J	E	I	G	P	J	N	Z	T
K	A	Q	R	A	W	N	Y	C	X	E	H
R	D	G	P	U	C	C	I	N	I	W	M

SEE ANSWER 20

LEVEL • TOUGH

By taking a sector and finding its pair in the diagram the name of four scientists can be found. Who are they?

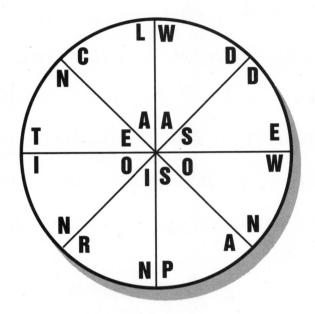

SEE ANSWER 46

PUZZLE 14

In a jar you have collected $14.41. It is made up of an equal number of four coins of different denominations from 1c, 5c, 10c, 25c, 50c and $1. Any four of the coins may be in the jar. How many of each coin is there and what are their respective values?

SEE ANSWER 61

LEVEL • TOUGH

PUZZLE 15

In a library the number of copies of books by certain authors is shown here. How many Agatha Christie books are there?

Emily Bronte
50

Stephen King
65

Jane Austen
25

Agatha
Christie
?

SEE ANSWER 24

PUZZLE 16

Rearrange each of the following groups to find four names.
Which one is the odd one out?

VADY   LIVVAID   RUICE

CHIMEDARES

SEE ANSWER 7

Michel, Noel and Olivier went on a spending spree in India over four days. Michel spent one-fifth of his money on the first day, then two-fifths of the remainder the second day, a half of what was left the next day and one-third of what was left on the last day. Noel spent a half, a third, two-thirds and a half of the remainder on the final day. Olivier spent a third, a half, a quarter and two-thirds on the final day. If Michel started with 100 rupees and after the fourth day they all had the same amount left, how much did they spend between them?

SEE ANSWER 30

Can you calculate which numbers will replace A, B and C in the diagram below?

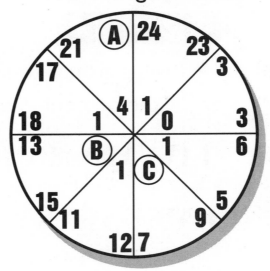

SEE ANSWER 37

PUZZLE 19

Three American states are merged together here.
Which are they?

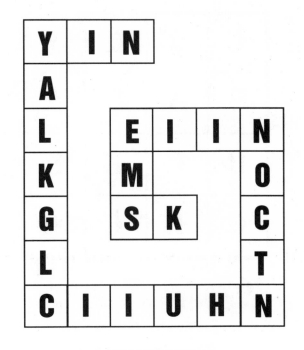

SEE ANSWER 54

PUZZLE 20

If Bacardi is written YXZXOAF in a certain code,
what are the drinks listed below?

a) **DFK ?**
b) **ORJ ?**
c) **TEFPHBV ?**
d) **ZXJMXOF ?**
e) **PLRQEBOK ZLJCLOQ ?**
f) **SLAHX ?**

SEE ANSWER 26

LEVEL · TOUGH

Each letter in the diagram has a value. What number should replace the question mark?

C	B	A	A	
B	A	B	A	46
B	C	B	B	59
C	B	C	C	
62	?			

SEE ANSWER 44

PUZZLE 22

This clock was correct at midnight (A) but began to lose 3½ minutes per hour from that moment. It stopped 1½ hours ago (B). The clock runs for less than 24 hours. What is the correct time now?

A   **B**

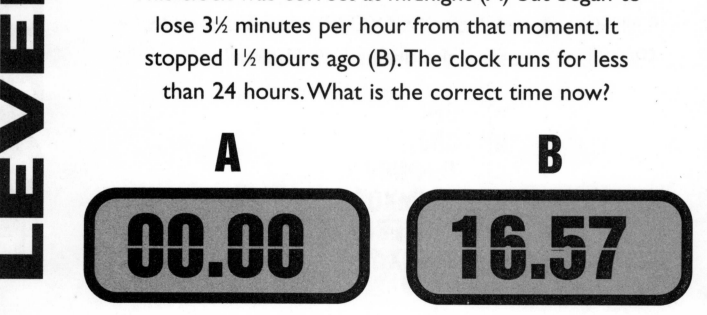

00.00   16.57

SEE ANSWER 59

PUZZLE 23

Place one letter in the middle of this diagram. The name of a composer can then be rearranged from each straight line of letters. Who are the four composers?

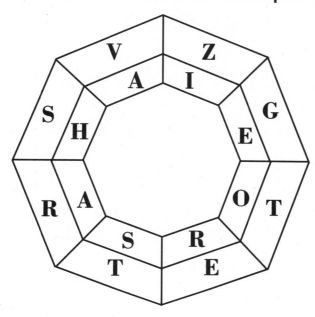

SEE ANSWER 32

PUZZLE 24

The arrows spiral anti-clockwise (counterclockwise) from the top left corner to the middle. In which direction should the missing arrow point?

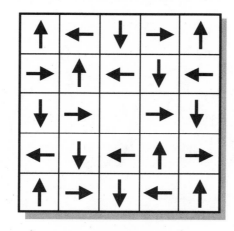

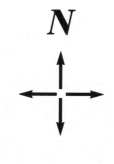

SEE ANSWER 16

Assume you are using a basic calculator and press the numbers in order replacing each question mark with a mathematical sign. Plus, minus, multiply and divide can each be used once only. What are the highest and lowest totals possible?

a) 3 ? 5 ? 5 ? 1 ? 1 =

b) 5 ? 4 ? 6 ? 9 ? 9 =

c) 8 ? 1 ? 3 ? 7 ? 2 =

d) 9 ? 3 ? 6 ? 7 ? 1 =

SEE ANSWER 2

(PUZZLE 26)

Four interlinked gear wheels with arrows on them start in the position shown below. If the largest wheel is rotated clockwise for 7 rotations, what directions will the arrows point on the 3 smaller wheels. The number of teeth on each wheel is given on the diagram.

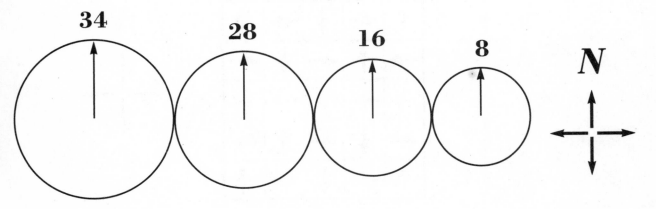

SEE ANSWER 39

Can you rearrange the numbers 1, 2, 3, 3 and 4 in this sum to give the answers shown?

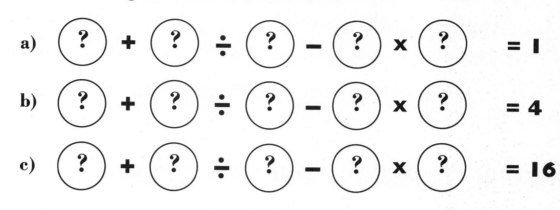

a) ? + ? ÷ ? – ? x ? = 1

b) ? + ? ÷ ? – ? x ? = 4

c) ? + ? ÷ ? – ? x ? = 16

SEE ANSWER 56

PUZZLE 28

4A	1E	5B		3D	1B	5E	3C	3B
2B	5C	3D		2A	4A	2D	2E	4D

The wordframe above, when filled with the correct letters, will give the name of a singer. The letters are arranged in the grid below. There are two possible letters to fill each square of the wordframe, one correct, the other incorrect. Who is the singer?

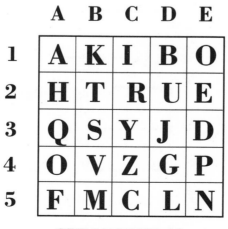

	A	B	C	D	E
1	A	K	I	B	O
2	H	T	R	U	E
3	Q	S	Y	J	D
4	O	V	Z	G	P
5	F	M	C	L	N

SEE ANSWER 18

LEVEL • TOUGH

The letters of five American cities are written here but their order has been mixed up and one letter is missing from each. Rearrange the letters and replace the letters missing. The missing letters will give the name of a sixth city when placed together. What are the six cities?

PIMSHE THURGPBST TROLNPD TROLABIE LIPPHEADAHL

SEE ANSWER 42

PUZZLE 30

Which of these is not a view of the same box?

A

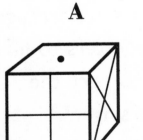

B

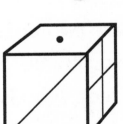

C

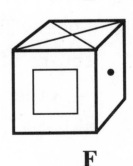

D

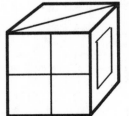

E

F

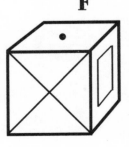

SEE ANSWER 63

PUZZLE 31

In a small orchard one-third of all the fruit falls from the trees on the first day. The next day a quarter of what is left falls and on the third day one-third of the remaining fruit falls. On the fourth day half the remaining fruit falls leaving 422 pieces of fruit still on the trees. How many pieces of fruit have fallen?

SEE ANSWER 25

PUZZLE 32

How many squares and rectangles can you find in this puzzle?

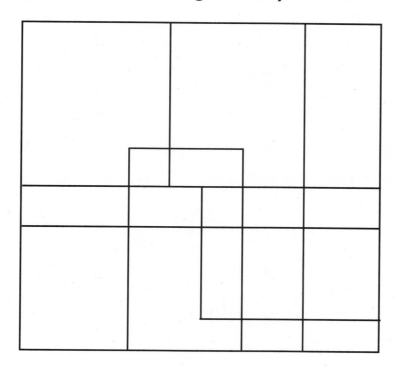

SEE ANSWER 1

LEVEL • TOUGH

Given the information in balances 1 and 2, and each same letter has the same value, will the right-hand tray in balance 3 move up or down?

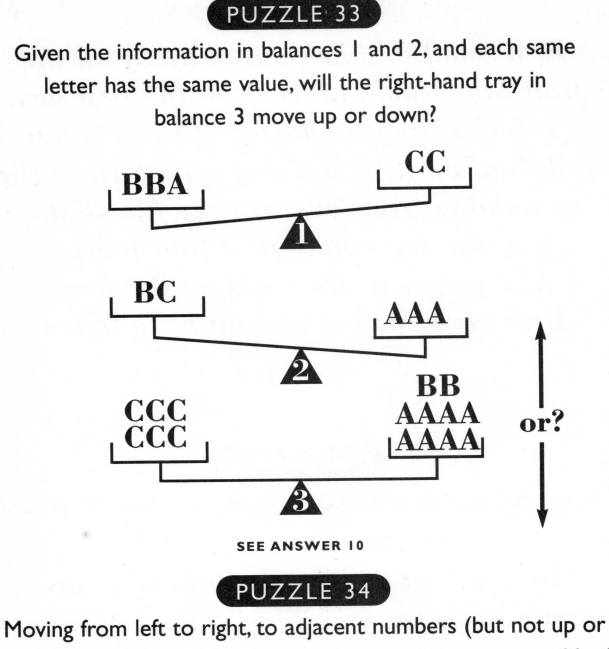

SEE ANSWER 10

PUZZLE 34

Moving from left to right, to adjacent numbers (but not up or down), what are the maximum and minimum scores possible if there are 5 ways of scoring 106. What is the missing number?

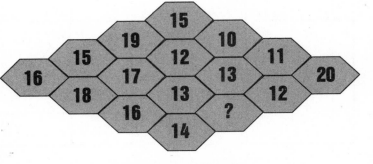

SEE ANSWER 45

LEVEL • TOUGH

PUZZLE 35

Rearrange these number tiles in a 3 x 3 grid so that each pair of adjacent numbers add up to 23.

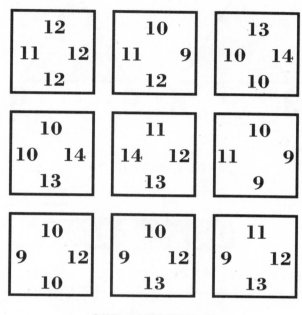

SEE ANSWER 60

PUZZLE 36

In a basket of fruit there are 7 more apples than bananas and 2 more oranges than bananas. There are 2 more pears than peaches and 2 more oranges than pears. The number of bananas added to the number of pears is 13. How many items of fruit are in the basket?

SEE ANSWER 15

LEVEL • TOUGH

89

What is the missing number?

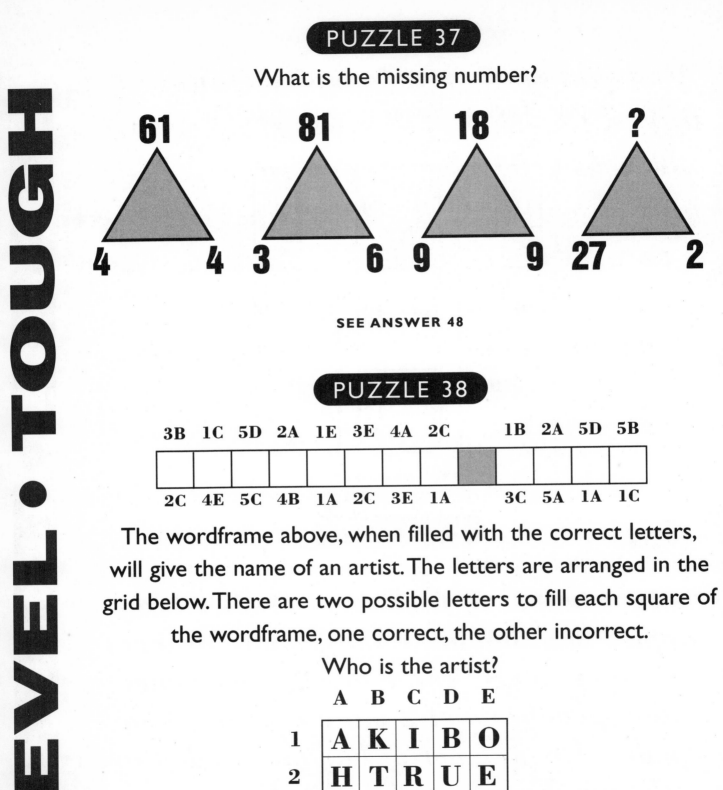

SEE ANSWER 48

PUZZLE 38

3B	1C	5D	2A	1E	3E	4A	2C		1B	2A	5D	5B

| 2C | 4E | 5C | 4B | 1A | 2C | 3E | 1A | | 3C | 5A | 1A | 1C |

The wordframe above, when filled with the correct letters, will give the name of an artist. The letters are arranged in the grid below. There are two possible letters to fill each square of the wordframe, one correct, the other incorrect.

Who is the artist?

	A	B	C	D	E
1	A	K	I	B	O
2	H	T	R	U	E
3	Q	S	D	J	D
4	O	V	Z	G	A
5	A	M	C	L	N

SEE ANSWER 53

LEVEL • TOUGH

PUZZLE 39

A car has four gear wheels which are linked together. The largest wheel has 88 teeth and the others have 32, 24 and 16 respectively. If the large wheel is rotated through 16 revolutions what will be the average number of revolutions of all four gear wheels?

SEE ANSWER 23

PUZZLE 40

By taking a sector and finding its pair in the diagram the name of four composers can be found. Who are they?

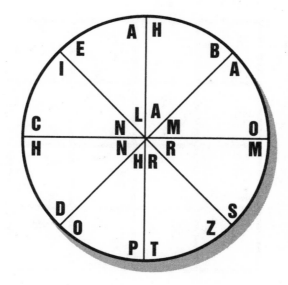

SEE ANSWER 9

PUZZLE 41

In a supermarket there were six more people standing in line at checkout desk 1 than at checkout desk 2, and five less at checkout desk 2 than at checkout desk 3. Checkout desk 5 had two more people waiting than at checkout desk 4, and there were two more standing at checkout desk 3 than at checkout desk 5. The total number of people at checkout desks 2 and 5 was nine. How many people were at each checkout desk?

SEE ANSWER 6

PUZZLE 42

Which two boxes in the diagram have the same symbols?

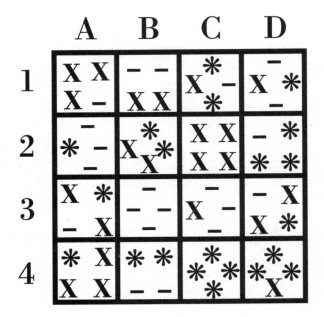

SEE ANSWER 33

This clock was correct at midnight, showing the time on clock A, but began to lose 3½ minutes per hour from that moment. It stopped 2½ hours ago showing the time on clock B. The clock runs for less than 24 hours. What is the correct time now?

A

00.00

B

13.11

SEE ANSWER 3

PUZZLE 44

How many triangles and rectangles can you find in the following shape?

SEE ANSWER 28

LEVEL · TOUGH

LEVEL • TOUGH

PUZZLE 45

There is A$48.60 in a slot machine in a bar in the Australian Outback. It is made up of an equal number of four coins of different denominations: A$2, A$1, 50c, 20c, 10c and 5c. How many of each of the four coins are there and what are their respective values?

SEE ANSWER 38

PUZZLE 46

What number should replace the question mark?

6	8	4	2
9	7	5	7
3	5	8	6
1	4	9	?

SEE ANSWER 55

The names of three scientists are merged together here.
Who are they?

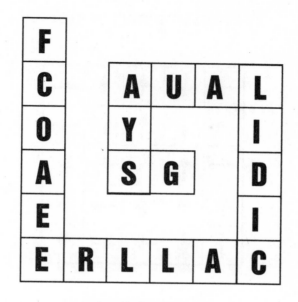

SEE ANSWER 17

PUZZLE 48

How many squares and rectangles can be found
in this diagram?

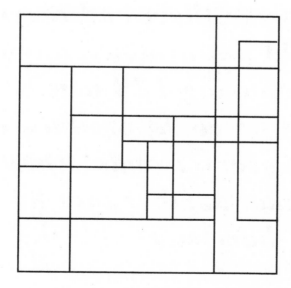

SEE ANSWER 58

LEVEL · TOUGH

PUZZLE 49

The arrows spiral clockwise from the top left corner to the middle. In which direction should the missing arrow point?

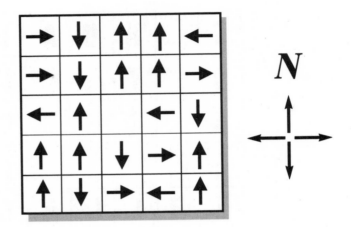

SEE ANSWER 14

PUZZLE 50

That miser has recycled an unknown number of crayon sticks. After he has made new ones from them and recycled those until he could not produce any more he has finished producing 133 new crayons from the ends. If he could produce one crayon stick for every 7 ends, what was the minimum number that he could have started with?

SEE ANSWER 41

Planet A is in line with planet B and the sun. Planet A completes an orbit of the sun in 200 years and planet B completes an orbit of the sun in 75 years. When will they next fall in line with each other and the sun?

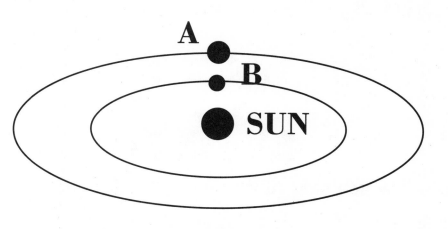

SEE ANSWER 62

PUZZLE 52

A rocket has a constant acceleration during each stage. Stage one moves it from zero to 1500 km/h in 30 seconds and then it takes 90 seconds to reach 2500 km/h. If it stays at this speed for the next 75 seconds what will be the rocket's average speed from launch?

SEE ANSWER 22

LEVEL · TOUGH

The names of three authors are written here, but the vowels have been missed out. Replace the vowels to discover the three names. Who are they?

CHRLSDCKNS   MRKTWN   RLDDHL

SEE ANSWER 36

PUZZLE 54

Can you tell which side (if one is) of the fourth set of scales is heavier, if the first three scales are in perfect balance?

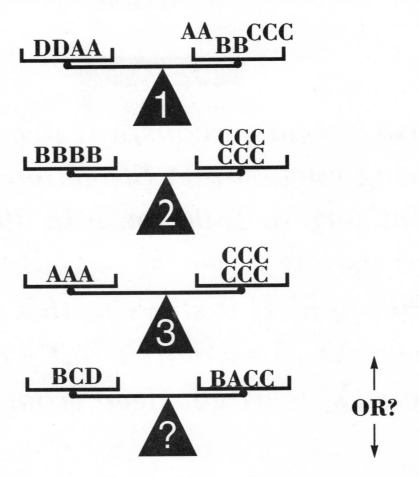

SEE ANSWER 64

PUZZLE 55

Can you see how many squares and rectangles
can be found in this diagram?

SEE ANSWER 19

PUZZLE 56

A store sells red and blue T-shirts. On the first day one-third of each are sold but on the following day one-half of the remaining red T-shirts and one-fifth of the remaining blue T-shirts are sold. The third day sees sales of two-fifths of the red and one-third of the blue T-shirts and on the final day one-third of the remaining red T-shirts plus one-quarter of the remaining blue T-shirts are sold. This leaves the store with twice as many blue T-shirts as red left. If the store started with 270 red T-shirts, how many blue T-shirts were there at the start.

SEE ANSWER 13

An array of red, green and blue lights change every 10 seconds. Half of all red lights turn to green and half to blue, half of the blue lights change to green and the other half change to red and half of the green lights change to red but the other half stay green. If there are 640 lights, and at the start 320 are red, 192 are blue and the remainder green, how many lights will be blue after 21 seconds?

SEE ANSWER 8

PUZZLE 58

Some letters have been omitted from this alphabet.
Use the missing letters to form the name of a scientist.

ABCDHJKOPQRSTUVWXYZ

SEE ANSWER 47

PUZZLE 59

Here is a (fictional!) list of the amount of time certain British Prime Ministers were in office. So, how many days was Margaret Thatcher Prime Minister of Britain?

Edward Heath 1000 days
James Callaghan 1200 days
Harold Wilson 601 days
Winston Churchill 302 days

SEE ANSWER 51

PUZZLE 60

Which boxes in the diagram have the same symbols?

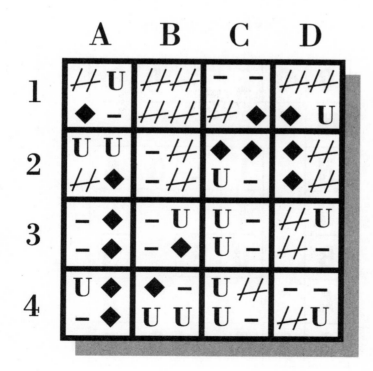

SEE ANSWER 29

LEVEL • TOUGH

101

PUZZLE 61

By taking a sector and finding its pair in the diagram the name of four presidents can be found. Who are they?

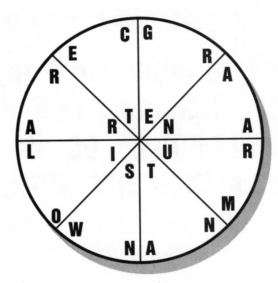

SEE ANSWER 34

PUZZLE 62

The names of three artists are merged together here. Who are they?

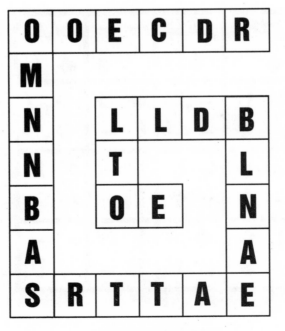

SEE ANSWER 49

PUZZLE 63

The arrows run diagonally from the top left corner
to the bottom right corner. In which direction
should the missing arrow point?

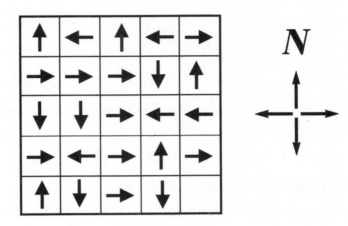

SEE ANSWER 21

PUZZLE 64

*In an athletics season Carl Lewis runs
thirty-six 100-m races in an average time of
10.09 seconds. He also runs twenty-four
200-m races at an average time of
20.21 seconds. In the long jump his average
run up is 35 m and his average time in
twelve jumps for this is 4.2 seconds.
Over the season what is his average
speed in m/s?*

SEE ANSWER 5

EASY ANSWERS

1. International.

2.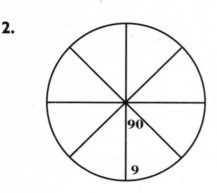

    In each segment, consecutive outer numbers alternate, odd going clockwise, even in the opposite direction. The two outer numbers are then multiplied to give each inner number.

3. The minimum is 40, the maximum 51, and 40 can be achieved 3 ways.

4. Venus, Saturn, Mars, Pluto.

5. You have 7 each of 1 cent, 10 cents, 25 cents and 50 cents.

6. 10. Alphabetical position of first letter.

7. A.

8. 7. The top line plus the middle line gives the bottom line.

9.

10. 7.40 (20 minutes to 8). The clock moves forward one-and-a-half hours each time.

11. 5 As.

12. 500 km. The number of consonants in the city name is multiplied by 100 to give the distance.

13.

```
P   O   P
O   N   E
P   E   T
```

14.

```
O   A   K
A   R   E
K   E   Y
```

15. 41. ★ = 5; ○ = 10; □ = 13.

16. 5 am.

17.

The top and left numbers are multiplied to give the middle. They are added to give the right.

18. 35. $x = 7$; ✚ = 9; □ = 12.

19. The missing letter is A, and the currencies are Franc, Dollar, Rand, and Peseta.

20. Starting from the top and moving clockwise, adjacent sectors give Alaska, Nevada, Oregon and Kansas.

21. 4 pm or 1600 hours.

22. Coffee, Tea, Sugar and Milk. Sugar is the odd one out, the other three are all drinks.

23. 6 ways.

24. 87 squares.

25. 51. The Roman numeral values in each name are added together.

26. George Michael.

27. 10 triangles.

28.

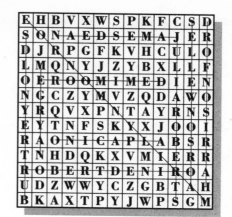

29. B.

30. 3A and 3D.

31. 2D and 3C.

32. 35 new bars of soap.

33. Bowl and blow.

34. 2 Cs.

35. Diana Ross.

36. Adult, Coach, Hello, Empty, Eight, Basic and Piano. The missing word is Dolphin.

37. The missing letter is O. The artists are Constable, Picasso and Monet.

38. Paper.

39. 45. Adam ate 12, Belinda ate 4, Chris ate 11, Dawn ate 8 and Eddie ate 10.

40. 10. They are the units used in Roman numerals.

41. 40 triangles.

42. Mississippi.

43. a) +, ÷, x, −.
    b) +, x, −, ÷.

44. 13 m.

45. New York.

46. Volkswagen.

47. Robert has 4 of each of 1 centime, 5 centimes, 10 centimes and 50 centimes.

48. Marilyn Monroe.

49. 3 ways.

50. 2001. The Roman numerals in each name are added together to give the page number.

51. South. The series is: South, East, West, North.

52. Muhammad Ali.

53. 1D and 2A.

54. There will be 20 red, 12 green and 32 blue.

55. B.

56. D.

57.

58. Simple Minds and Led Zeppelin.

59. Porsche, Bentley and Ferrari.

60. Jupiter.

61. 19. The previous two numbers are added together.

62. C.

SOLUTIONS TO MEDIUM PUZZLES

1.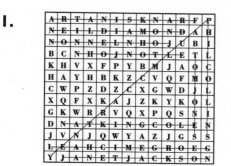

2. 9 each of 1 pfennig, 5 pfennig, 10 pfennig and 1 Deutschmark.

3.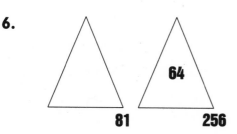

   Subtract the two bottom numbers from the top one and put the answer in the middle of each triangle.

4. A = 10; B = 1. The sum of each of the segments is double the sum of the opposite segments.

5. B1 and A4.

6.

   In each case the left number is the square of the top one, the middle number is the cube of it and the right number is to the power of four.

7. T. The series comprises every third consonant.

8. 24. In each name a vowel is worth four and a consonant is worth two. These are added together to give the number of hit records.

9. 1.20. The time moves on half an hour, one hour, 1½ hours and finally two hours.

10. 10 minutes to 3. The amount of time the clock moves forward halves each time: it moves forward two hours, then one hour then half an hour and finally a quarter of an hour.

11. The missing letter is R to give Gretzky, Navratilova, Christie and Sampras.

12. West. The order is west, east, north, east, west, south.

13. 110. O = 27; X = 28.

14. Arizona, Oklahoma, Indiana, Oregon. The new state is Ohio.

15. Newark, Boston, Albany and Austin can be found in alternate segments starting from the top of the diagram.

MEDIUM ANSWERS

107

16.

17. 21. The others are all prime numbers.

17. 36. Multiply the three outer numbers together and divide the answer by 10.

18. Five ways.

19. There would be 6 defects in each assembly (0.3%).

20. C.

21. 7. The totals of the columns form a series: the first column totals 6, the second totals 12, the third totals 18 and the fourth totals 24.

22. Annie scored 95, Bertie scored 20, Charlie scored 88, Donny scored 35 and Ernie scored 62 marks.

23. 50 km/h.

24. 3. The totals of the rows form a series. The top row totals 5, the second row totals 10, the third row totals 15 and the fourth row totals 20.

25. Maximum = 200; Minimum = 166; 171 = 5 ways.

26. 70 goals were scored. Angela scored 26, Betty scored 3, Christy scored 19, Daisy scored 8 and Eva scored 14.

27. Bangkok, Jakarta and Kowloon.

28. 193. A = 45, B = 48, C = 52.

29. Jordan, Becker and Berger are found by pairing opposite segments.

30. 64 candles.

31. A and T are missing from Budapest, Frankfurt, Manchester and Bucharest.

32. Portland.

33. 10. The Roman numerals in each state are added together.

34.

8 5　12 −3	4 −1　7 4	11 4　2 14
14 4　12 5	7 −1　4 6	−3 7　9 −3
6 9　4 8	5 7　12 3	14 −1　−1 4

35. Kroner, Dollar and Peseta can be found in opposite sectors.

36. Isaac Newton, Albert Einstein and Louis Pasteur.

37. $121. Aileen has $35, Bruce has $12, Charlotte has $30, Denis has $16 and Emily has $28.

38. Julia Roberts.

39.

36   32   16   9

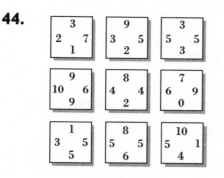

Adjacent wheels rotate clockwise, then the opposite way.

40. 4B and 3D.

41. 6 ways.

42. Nick Faldo.

43. 24 triangles.

44.

3 2 7 1	9 3 5 2	3 5 5 3
9 10 6 9	8 4 4 2	7 6 9 0
1 3 5 5	8 5 5 6	10 5 1 4

45. The girl's average speed was 3.2 km/h.

46.

9 10 2 6	9 10 8 5	8 4 8 2
6 6 8 5	8 4 7 6	10 5 5 3
7 5 7 4	6 5 6 2	9 6 4 3

47. Auckland, Brisbane and Canberra.

48. Robert De Niro.

49. Suzuki, Toyota, Daewoo, Nissan. Three letters appear in alternate sectors.

50.

M	I	L	W	A	U	K	E	E	I
A	B	C	J	X	K	X	H	T	P
T	U	Q	S	A	L	L	A	D	H
I	Q	S	Z	H	M	N	N	C	O
O	X	F	T	I	N	Z	N	G	E
R	H	B	A	I	V	B	A	H	N
T	P	M	C	W	N	Q	V	C	I
E	I	N	Q	C	J	K	A	J	X
D	I	B	X	N	O	T	S	O	B
C	H	I	C	A	G	O	Z	W	G

51. 7. Each small square of four numbers totals 23.

52. 154 candles.

53. 275 miles.

54. 8 rotations.

55. 2 pm.

56. 6 of each of 1p, 20p, 50p and £1.

57. Andy is 15, Beattie is 8, Carrie is 13, Danni is 10 and Elsie is 12.

58. 7.30 pm or 19.30 hours.

59. Sean Connery.

60. 35 triangles.

61. William Wordsworth.

62.

52   40   32   16

Adjacent wheels rotate clockwise, then the opposite way.

63. a) 8 ways; b) 4 ways; c) 2 ways; d) 2 ways.

64. 96 lengths.

SOLUTIONS TO TOUGH PUZZLES

TOUGH ANSWERS

1. 68 (remember, all squares are also rectangles!).

2. a) 39 (+ x − ÷) and −9 (− x + ÷ or − x ÷ +)
   b) 82.5 (− ÷ + x) and −67.5 (+ ÷ − x)
   c) 75 (÷ + x −) and −8 (+ ÷ − x)
   d) 84 (− + x ÷) and −20 (÷ − x +)

3. 16.30 (or 4.30 pm).

4. 50. The value of the first Roman numeral minus the value of the second in each city gives the amount.

5. 10.118 m/s.

6. 9 at checkout desk 1, 3 at desk 2, 8 at desk 3, 4 at desk 4 and 6 at desk 5.

7. Vivaldi, a composer. The others are Davy, Curie and Archimedes who are all scientists.

8. 80 lights will be blue.

9. Brahms, Mozart, Chopin and Handel are found in alternate segments.

10. The right side is heavier.

11. Oscar Wilde.

12. 1A and 4A.

13. 270 blue T-shirts.

14. West. The series goes: East, South, North, North, West.

15. 41. There are 12 apples, 5 bananas, 10 oranges, 6 peaches and 8 pears.

16. North. The order is: North, East, South, West.

17. Faraday, Celsius and Galileo.

18. Tom Jones.

19. 126 (remember, all squares are also rectangles).

20.

21. East. The series is: North, West, East, South, East.

22. The rocket's average speed is 2000 k/mh.

23. 51⅔ (51.666) revolutions.

24. 50. A consonant is worth 10 and a vowel is worth –5. The sum of these gives the answer.

25. 2110.

26.
a) Gin
b) Rum
c) Whiskey
d) Campari
e) Southern Comfort
f) Vodka

Imagine the alphabet is written in order around a circle. Move three letters back each time to find each name.

27. 3.15. Time moves on 3 hours 20 minutes, 3 hours 15 minutes, 3 hours 10 minutes and finally 3 hours and 5 minutes.

28. 10 triangles, 17 rectangles.

29. 4A and 2C.

30. 532 rupees. Michel started with 100 rupees, Noel with 288 rupees and Olivier with 192 rupees. They all had 16 rupees remaining.

31. 2,560 left the warehouse and 2,080 were delivered.

32. The missing letter is L. The names are: Liszt, Elgar, Holst and Ravel.

33. 3A and 3D.

34. Starting at the top adjacent segments give Reagan, Truman, Wilson and Carter.

35. 5 ways.

36. Charles Dickens, Mark Twain and Roald Dahl.

37. A = 19; B = 4 and C = 4. In each sector, one outer number is a multiple of 3. The next one, going clockwise is a sequence of prime numbers. The middle is the square of the difference between the two numbers.

38. 27 each of 10c, 20c, 50c and A$1.

39.

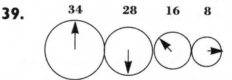

Adjacent wheels rotate clockwise, then the opposite way.

40. A (or 1). Letters replace numbers using an alphanumeric system (i.e. A = 1, B = 2, P = 16, Z = 26).

41. 799 crayon sticks.

42. Memphis, Pittsburgh, Portland, Baltimore and Philadelphia. The new city is Miami.

43. D. The diagonal lines continue, the four small shapes at the bottom become a large one and a four new small shapes go inside it.

44. 54. A = 9; B = 14; C = 17.

45. Maximum = 109; minimum = 101; ? = 10.

46. Opposite sectors give Darwin, Edison, Newton and Pascal.

47. Fleming.

48. 45. Multiply the bottom numbers and put the answer on top, with the digits reversed. 2 x 27 = 54; 54 becomes 45.

49. Rembrandt, Donatello and Constable.

50. Margaret Thatcher.

51. 1100 days. The Roman numerals in each name are added together.

52. 24. There are 8 yellow rose bushes, 2 orange, 6 pink, 3 white and 5 red.

53. Salvador Dali.

54. Kentucky, Michigan and Illinois.

55. 6. On each row the first and third numbers are added and the second number is deducted to give the fourth number.

56.
a) 3 3 4 1 2
b) 3 3 1 4 2
c) 3 3 1 2 4

57. 75 (remember, all squares are also rectangles!).

58. 87 (remember, all squares are also rectangles!).

59. 7.30 pm (or 19.30).

60.

10 10 14 13	10 9 12 13	12 11 12 12
10 9 12 10	10 11 9 12	11 14 12 13
13 10 14 10	11 9 12 13	10 11 9 9

61. 11 of 1c, 5c, 25c and $1.

62. 60 years.

63. E.

64. They are also in perfect balance. A = 4, B = 3, C = 2, D = 6.